Missouri

BY AMY VAN ZEE

The Child's World

Published by The Child's World®
1980 Lookout Drive • Mankato, MN 56003-1705
800-599-READ • www.childsworld.com

ACKNOWLEDGMENTS
The Child's World®: Mary Berendes, Publishing Director
The Design Lab: Design and production
Red Line Editorial: Editorial direction

PHOTO CREDITS: Mitch Aunger/Shutterstock Images, cover, 1, 3; Matt
Kania/Map Hero, Inc., 4, 5; Pete Hoffman/Shutterstock Images, 7; Clint
Spencer/iStockphoto, 9; iStockphoto, 10; Darren K. Fisher/Shutterstock
Images, 11; Kyu Oh/iStockphoto, 13; North Wind Picture Archives/
Photolibrary, 15; Michael Westhoff/iStockphoto, 17; AP Images, 19; Jeremy
Edwards/iStockphoto, 21; One Mile Up, 22; Quarter-dollar coin image from
the United States Mint, 22

LIBRARY OF CONGRESS CATALOGING-IN-PUBLICATION DATA
Van Zee, Amy.
  Missouri / by Amy Van Zee.
     p. cm.
  Includes bibliographical references and index.
  ISBN 978-1-60253-469-8 (library bound : alk. paper)
  1. Missouri—Juvenile literature. I. Title.

F466.3.V36 2010
977.8—dc22

                                    2010017927

Printed in the United States of America in Mankato, Minnesota.
July 2010
F11538

On the cover:
The Gateway
Arch is 630 feet
(192 m) tall.

CONTENTS

Geography

Let's explore Missouri! Missouri is in the central United States. It is part of the Midwest.

Missouri is called "the Show-Me State." It means that the people in the state will not just trust being told something. They want to be shown.

IOWA

Athens •

ILLINOIS

• Marceline   Hannibal •

Mississippi River

Missouri River

• Kansas City   • Marshall

• Lee's Summit   • Columbia

NORTH
WEST   EAST
SOUTH

Hermann •   Saint Louis •

Jefferson
City ★

KANSAS

Sullivan •

Sainte Genevieve •

MISSOURI

Cape Girardeau •

Springfield •

KENTUCKY

Marionville •

Ozark Mountains

• Branson

OKLAHOMA

TENNESSEE

ARKANSAS

Cities

Jefferson City is the capital of Missouri. Kansas City is Missouri's largest city. St. Louis, Springfield, and Columbia are other large cities.

Kansas City, Missouri, is home to about 450,000 people. ▶

Land

The Mississippi River is the eastern border of Missouri. The Missouri River flows through the state from west to east. Missouri also has **plains**, hills, and mountains. Some of the state's land is good for farming.

The Ozark Mountains are in southern Missouri. ▶

The Mississippi River and the Missouri River are the longest rivers in the United States. The Missouri River joins the Mississippi River just north of St. Louis.

Plants and Animals

Missouri has some forests. The flowering dogwood is Missouri's state tree. The bluebird is the state bird. It has blue feathers and a reddish-colored chest. The bluebird is a **symbol** for happiness. The white hawthorn blossom is the state flower. It is part of the rose family.

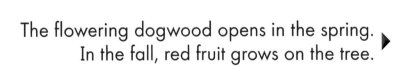

The flowering dogwood opens in the spring. ▶
In the fall, red fruit grows on the tree.

People and Work

Almost 6 million people live in Missouri. Many people live in or near large cities. Some people work in **manufacturing**, mining, or **transportation**. There are also many farms in Missouri.

Corn and wheat are grown in Missouri. Cattle and hogs are raised in the state.

Some people in Missouri make dairy products. ▶

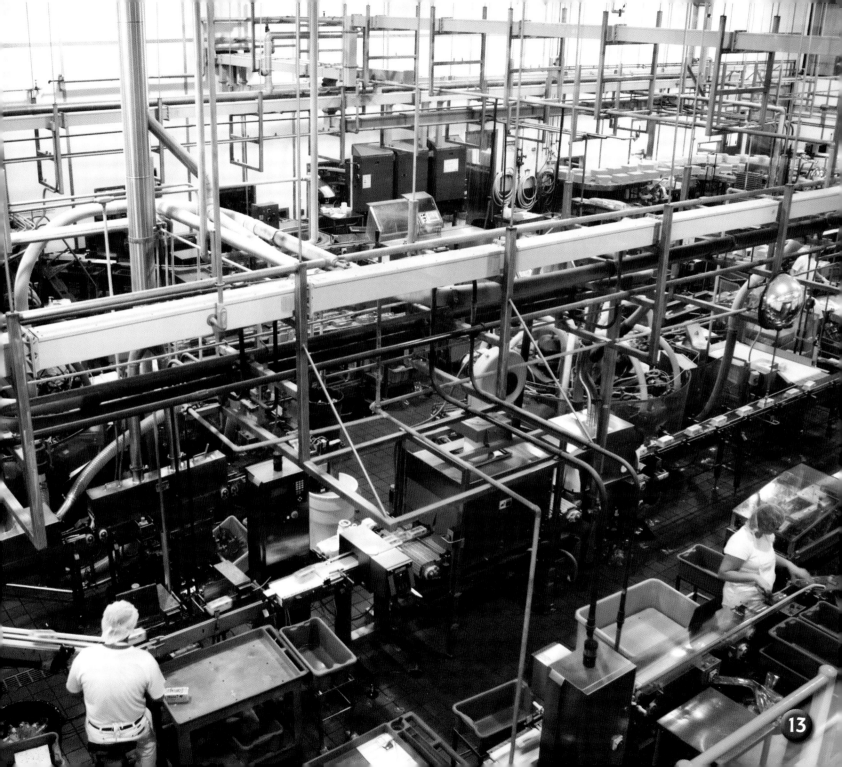

History

Explorers traveled on the Mississippi River into the Missouri area in the 1600s. At the time, many Native Americans lived there. In 1803, the area became part of the United States in the Louisiana Purchase. The land became the Missouri **Territory**. Missouri became the twenty-fourth state on August 10, 1821.

Shipping and transportation on the Mississippi ▶ River helped St. Louis grow during the 1800s.

Explorers Meriwether Lewis and William Clark explored the western United States in the early 1800s. They began and ended their travels in St. Louis.

Ways of Life

Missouri has art and history **museums**. People also enjoy many outdoor activities, including fishing. The Missouri State Fair is a **popular** event held in August. People can listen to music and see art, **parades**, and animals.

This woman canoes on a river in the Ozark Mountains area. ▶

Famous People

Writer Mark Twain was born in Missouri. Inventor George Washington Carver was born and raised in Missouri. Former U.S. President Harry Truman was also born in the state. Walt Disney spent much of his childhood in Missouri.

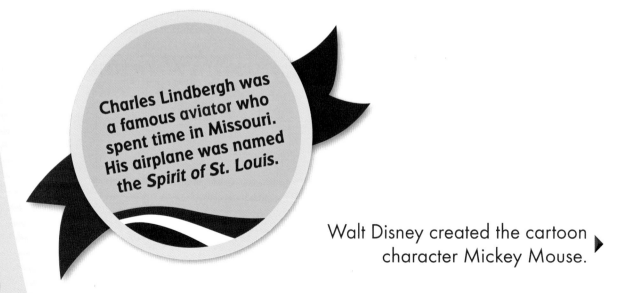

Charles Lindbergh was a famous aviator who spent time in Missouri. His airplane was named the *Spirit of St. Louis*.

Walt Disney created the cartoon character Mickey Mouse. ▶

Disney was born in 1901 and spent much of his childhood on a farm in Marceline, Missouri.

Famous Places

The Gateway Arch in St. Louis is one of Missouri's most famous places. Visitors can go to the top of the tall arch. The Mark Twain Boyhood Home & Museum in Hannibal was where the writer grew up. Visitors to the Ozark Mountains area can see streams, rivers, and animals.

About one million people ride to the top ▶
of the Gateway Arch each year.

State Symbols

Seal

Two grizzly bears are on Missouri's state seal. They stand for bravery. Go to childsworld.com/links for a link to Missouri's state Web site, where you can get a firsthand look at the state seal.

Flag

Missouri's state flag became official in 1913. It has twenty-four stars to show that Missouri was the twenty-fourth state.

Quarter

The Missouri state quarter honors explorers Lewis and Clark. The quarter came out in 2003.

Glossary

arch (ARCH): An arch is a curved structure. The Gateway Arch is in Missouri.

aviator (AY-vee-ay-tur): An aviator is a person who flies airplanes. Charles Lindbergh was a famous aviator who spent time in Missouri.

manufacturing (man-yuh-FAK-chur-ing): Manufacturing is the task of making items with machines. Some people in Missouri work in manufacturing.

museums (myoo-ZEE-umz): Museums are places where people go to see art, history, or science displays. Many museums are in Missouri.

parades (puh-RAYDZ): Parades are when people march to honor holidays. Visitors to the Missouri State Fair can see parades.

plains (PLAYNZ): Plains are areas of flat land that do not have many trees. Some of Missouri's land is plains.

popular (POP-yuh-lur): To be popular is to be enjoyed by many people. The Missouri State Fair is a popular event.

seal (SEEL): A seal is a symbol a state uses for government business. The Missouri state seal has two grizzly bears on it.

symbol (SIM-bul): A symbol is a picture or thing that stands for something else. The bluebird is a symbol for happiness.

territory (TAYR-uh-tor-ee): A territory is a piece of land that is controlled by another country. Missouri was a part of the Missouri Territory before it became a state.

transportation (trans-pur-TAY-shun): Transportation is moving people or things from one place to another. People in Missouri work in transportation.

Further Information

Books

Ruffin, Frances E. *The Gateway Arch*. Milwaukee, WI: Weekly Reader Early Learning Library, 2006.

Taylor-Butler, Christine. *Missouri*. New York: Children's Press, 2005.

Young, Judy. *S is for Show Me: A Missouri Alphabet*. Chelsea, MI: Sleeping Bear Press, 2001.

Web Sites

Visit our Web site for links about Missouri: *childsworld.com/links*

Note to Parents, Teachers, and Librarians: We routinely verify our Web links to make sure they are safe and active sites. So encourage your readers to check them out!

Index